PREFACE

This book was written to aid on the feeling of those who have been longing to be on their own in business and developing entrepreneur spirit this book have it unique side as it torch on every aspect of mental development toward human capacity building and entrepreneur goal it cover eight chapter, with their own subheading that you will fine time in your reading.

It chapter dealth very well in business development and will help you to draw a blue print in starting your own business.

Action is behind the writing of this book if at the end of reading this book and you have not taken action that mean the good of this books have not been put into action yet.

I wish you as you take the part of life and destiny into your own hand.

Happy reading.

ACKNOWLEDGEMENT

I want to thank all those who stand by me through all this length of time that I use in writing this book during the good time and the bad time and their unflinching support they gave me when I need them mostly. thank you very much and may God bless you all.

COPYRIGHT

TABLE OF CONTENT

CHAPTER 5: (INSTINCT iv)

INCORPORATION
CUT DOWN TAX AND BURDEN ON THE WAY YOU REGISTER YOUR BUSINESS
EITHER PARTNERSHIP
Or either Limited liability company
Or Either Unlimited
Or Corporation (Corp)
Use proper legal framework cut cost on business burden

CHAPTER 6
EXPANSION & PARTNERSHIP
1.   Expand your business concept far and wide
2.   Form partnership to drive your business idea

CHAPTER 7: TAKING YOUR BUSINESS TO PUBLIC DOMAN
1.   Initiate (IPO) initial public offer & private placement
2.   Study customer database and consumer index
3.   Establish customer help desk

CHAPTER 8: CORPORATE TAX SYSTEM AND INSURANCE
1.   Draw a easy blue print on matter concerning tax
2.   Insurance to cover every lope hole and unexpected occurrence

EIGHT INSTINCT OF BUSINESS INTILIGENCE

CHAPTER 1

STRATEGY IN ALL FACET OF OPERATION AND MANAGEMENT

COVER AREA OF INVENTION

In seem to be that you might have bypass so many intention before you get this one the intuition of taking you first step into the domain of starting from this corridor show that you about inqniting a revolution.

Congratulation once more for taking this giant stride.

The question I ask most people at time, who happing to go through this step is that? What are your area of expertises? Now the step you take to discover core area of expertise are enomous and huge some and them, putting them into technical aspect become more harder for achiever and later become easier when you know what you are doing.

In every critical step you take to unleash this, you must have a finding and the finding include:

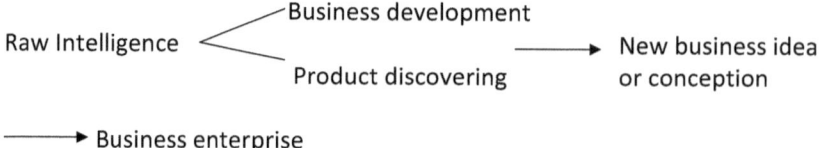

Your new business finding will look small on the board but will start gradually developing into big business idea and later become an enterprise.

Putting this step in order involve, you must take your finding into the library to make your first research your finding should include the birth of your new business conception, and formulate this formation.

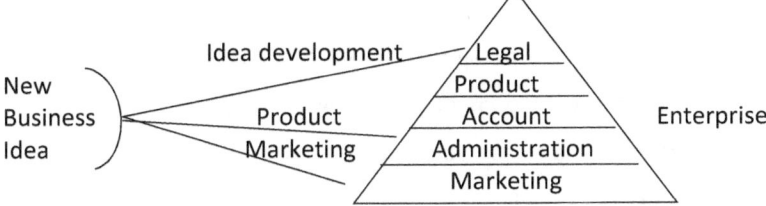

ask the Librian to help you out with books that torch on relevant field of business you intend to go into don't be afraid to ask because this people very nice and will be ready to help you out now your have to do next finding and should be various institute that offer the studies on the type of various business idea you intend to go into. If it is on raw material, then the institute of raw material and entrepreneur studies will be ready to extend their helping hand to you:

1) You should book appointment with them or the relevant person in that organization.
2) If they discard your invitation at first place don't feel discourage, but try again or try another person
3) Take a pen and notebook to put down every point in the interview.
4) Try to know what they go through, their challenges, and the cost they incurred trying run their business on daily basis

PROPER BUSINESS FINDING

Before you even dive into the new business you invented.

You should take every time to study every critical aspect of business from beginning to the end of development. You should always consider what make this business to be different from any other one people are doing then you ask yourself business? How big is the market? What should I do different from my rival? Do have the resources to carryout along all this tax all this should be put into y our proper business finding.

IN PRODUCT DEVELOPMENT

The unique side of this all is the product your business conception must cover the product and it inception and development to the finish.

Now, how do you want people to see your product? Is the package all done well and different from your closet rival.

Now think of the product that you want to develop from the inception to the finish the raw material that you will use, will be willing blended and follow various process to develop to actualize your product conception.

The next is to package it very neatly into container and should be done different from your rival and competitor brand your product in a good order so that it will meet international standard.

So as to enable your product to be consume in the international market and remember not only on the local market, if you must win the heart of your international consumer too and to win against your closing rival too.

IN BUSINESS ADMINISTRATION AND DEVELOPMENT

One good thing for you to do is for you to organize the system and also to lead it, but how to carryout this task? Can you really lead or be a leader?

The structure of your system determined weather the business is going to be a profitable one by being up and running.

I quite agree to this system, because most people approach their business with different business sense and system and make their business to fail very fast you must structure your business to involve, and must be like this system.

And those who should be on the helm of leadership should include

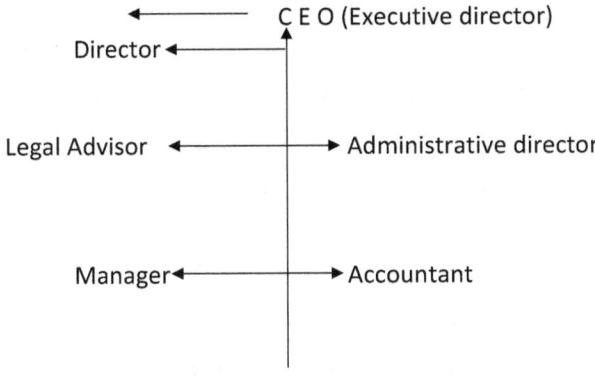

Member of Staff

1. The duty of CEO include drawing a roadmap and a blueprint on how the business should be run on a day to day basis.

2. Initiate and delegate responsibility

3. Hold weakly or monthly meeting to improve each department output.

4.   And see to the end user that the job is being carryout and executed.

Each department and personnel have its role to play in the area of administration, production marketing, accountant, and legal advisor the director delegate their own task to the employee and this responsibility pass down to the junior worker and member of staff to execute it how does all this fall down to you? You being a smaller business person, first and foremost you have to setup your system.

1.   Use legal advisor to help you out in all area of legal issue, because it will help you to cut cost on employee related cost by employing on lawyer to do the job for you

2.   Being that your business is still small, you can employ the service and hand of an accountant on a part time basis to carryout the job for you.
     I do have tremendous respect for accountant they know what you have, and know what you need to do to make tremendous more money for you and they will help you to make money and achieve your aim.

3.   Employ that every aspect of the system is put in place in the area of marketing, administration product development, account, legal, so as for you to achieve maximum input.

IN ALL AREA OF MARKETING AND DISTRIBUTION

Marketing is the life blood of any business growth and being done in many different ways the broad specialty of marketing goes very deep into various distribution and direct market sale.

But, in which one you decided to us is all left to be utilize in full by you to achieve your aim marketing is done in a different way and in the area of:

(1) Telemarketing (2) Media (3) Media print (4) Distributorship (5) Direct sale.

For you to reach your audience event more, you have to reach into their deep into mind, how do buy into this? Is by you doing marketing and advertising for you to be able to reach your set objective and business conception you must formulate how you intend reach your customer.

Is by doing advertising, media print, or telemarketing? Or just by direct sale.

Remember for you stand clear and remain different in the mind of your consumer you must:

1)   Formulate the way you plan to market your product.

2)   Do you marketing and distribution differently from your closest rival

3)   Know what your competitor are up to yours should be different in the area of marketing.

4)   Rebrand and package your product differently

5)   Advertising on the media, and news print

6)   Use various means on distributorship

7)   Applied direct sale most time and promo to achieve set market target.

CHAPTER 2

ACQUISITION

CORPORATE TAKEOVER, FREE FROM DEPT

There are many good reasons why you might consider buying your first business. If you know how to spot the honey then the business would be very easy to catch. There are many business out there whose owner are ready to sell their share in full or enterprise to a whose be investor who are ready to buy in full or seventy to ninety percent stake in most of the enterprise whose owner is ready to sell or transfer full responsibility stake or in full ownership to the whose by investor. This business don't need themselves anymore, they need new investor to come in and acquire them to pump new blood and capital so as to revegorate it to a smooth and running new life to start afresh in a smooth operation their, how do you know when a business don't need itself anymore? Or when to buy? This when the need for thorough research come in, you have to always go to option or liquidation conference or meeting to know when a business would be due for sell. There are government agency, like the (BPE) (Bereau for public enterprise) that are saddle with the responsibility to sell public enterprise to whoseby investor or private entity or transferring full owner to those who are ready to buy into private entity.

You can take your finding or research to this meeting or conference to see how you can acquire your first business.

How your research doesn't end there, you need to observe everything or point and figure on why the business need to be sell your presence there will give you overall advantage to know what is on the prospectus how you have look very clear and deep in the prospectus to know the difference and what the business and term off or before investing, and also look into the critical angle what investor are looking for you have to also look in the dept profile that is when the need for you to look into the corporate financial structure, from beginning to finish.

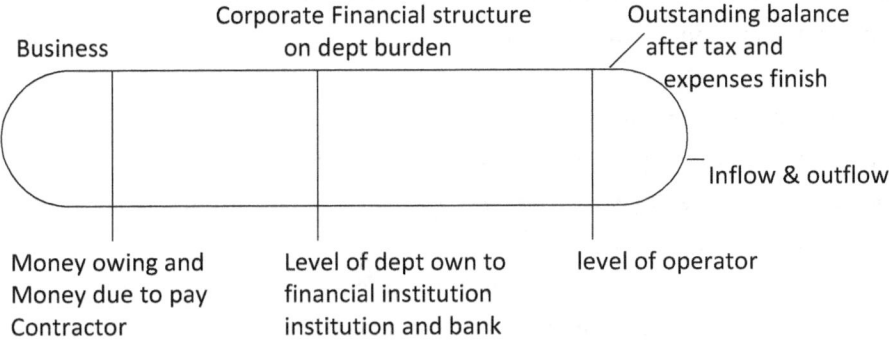

Corporate Financial structure on dept burden

Business

Outstanding balance after tax and expenses finish

Inflow & outflow

Money owing and Money due to pay Contractor

Level of dept own to financial institution institution and bank

level of operator

What you want to be observing is that:

1) Is overburden with dept after running expense or coming slowly out from recession

   Or Minimum dept profile

   Or Clean bill of good health from dept

2) How much does it hold on to contractor is too much to bring down on business operation

3) How much does it hold the bank and financial institute is it too much to bring down on operation and other dept burden.

4) You have know that cash inflow and outflow running expenses after tax and other operational cost before you can give it a clean bill of health.

CORPORATE TAKEOVER – FAIR BAIL OUT

One good thing is that, if you buy into it very well, you will reap very good investment bargain, but do you know weather that one good deal is a good bargain? Then information gathering will tell you weather you are good in a good buy, you have to gather your information as an investor and look very deep into the prospectus.

The business is slowing recouping from dept and the shareholder have all agree to sell hundred percent holding of the company and the director have also agree base on shareholder to liquidate it, and they call for memorandum of understanding of those who may want to look into it all may be interested into the deal.

Now before you even buy a business as such, you may want to be cautious, being that is slowly recouping from his dept, and that is what is prompting the reason for his sale, your may to want consider this something before putting money into it as an investor.

1)   You must consider the level of dept it is into.

2)   How much of your money that ready to go inside and bring it back to normal operation?

3)   Who are the whoseby investor and how much does it cost to clear up their holding?

4)   Is the money you have put into the deal is too much to recoup it back or have good beyond the level every investor would consider to much to invest into the project.

5)   Is the business still viable, and how much does it cost to put it back to his foot.

6)   Is the product still consumer friendly, so as for you to recoup the money you use buying the business.

CORPORATE TAKEOVER, BANKRUPTCY

Investor who take the risk in putting their money weather the deal become good or bad are only trying to see weather they can even bring out good thing from bad.

There are many company and business out there that are hundred percent fully into dept that about declaring bankruptcy or either closing shop for business, because of too much business dept in running high expense due to operational cost.

Buying a business from scratch and hundred percent into dept is riskers for an investor to want attempt, for any investor to do that, he must be very cautious, and use his parameter to know the most intricate aspect of the deal before investing.

Now, closing down shop and shutting down business due to high operation and high dept profile mean much there are you ready to sacrifice much to bring back this business to it normal state? How much of its risk can your afford to buy back? Before you ever think of buying into a business is that business still any a foast to whoseby investor.

Now, the structure of the burden on dept cannot be carry all alone by you the investor you have to look into the level of how much dept it is into, that is why need not go it alone by yourself. You need other investor too, that is why you need those investor so as for you to share the responsibility on dept burden so as for them to carry too by sharing some part of the investment with them and with some state too.

After you have succeeded in buying the business with your core investor, now you need do (proper management structured adjustment) you will need to cut down on surplus that you always using to pay contractor and want to cut down on downsizing of your employee strength to minimize cost on operational burden and dept burden. Rearrange or call for meeting with your banker for them to reschedule the money and dept your own so as for you to state the course forward.

WHAT YOU NEED TO LOOK FOR BEFORE YOUR FIRST BUSINESS AND FRANCISE

If you contemplate on buyer your first business you must wait and consider one thing, you may want to know what are you gain and what you stand to benefit from the deak sow before ever think of taking that step, you want to know the gain, now this are what you should be looking for.

1) By you looking into the prospectus you want know net is saving you the benefit of new market share (2) does the business come with a lot of incentive (3) are you making a lot of percent gain in the area of sharing with your fellow investor.

MINIMIZE YOUR RISK AND MAXIMIZE INCOME CASHFLOW IN THE END USE SIDE OF CORPORATE BUYBACK

Now that you have put all infrastructure in place, and still trying to bring down on corporate risk, and the business have recoup and become back on his feet.

You then decided to sell your hundred percent holding that you have in that business to core investor. Then you put on a memorandum of understanding to that effect, and bidding process began.

Then what you should be taking note of is that you may want to know, during the first time you bought the holding as an investor, how much does it cost you? How was the interest them? What do you stand to gain as an investor.

You intend selling your h0lding now, because you don't want to be on the controlling side for too long trying to:

Controlling risk

Controlling employee

Controlling operational cost

And other expenses

And you want to let off by minizing your risk and take good control of your gain for sell....

Try to know your gain and the reason for doing so, know the incentive and benefit and remain open in every side to know what you should be doing.

CHAPTER 3

RISK CONTROL

CONTROL UPTREND

"Risk" is a word that connote so many different tissue of financial volotilebity of system of management risk is everywhere in business and grow and become empire of its own if not properly manage.

If a business fail to pat up proper management risk system. The risk will certainly grow and become uncontrollable, the trend might even been worse if you didn't care to put your risk under proper control and maintenance.

In most case, people are the causes of half of the percent of high risk and this all bring us to the issue of altitude control and checkup at time you will hear people saying that they don't want to be in risk or even take risk in actualizing their dream but how can you be in business without going through risk the big issue here is that people don't understand the concept of the all thing at all the reason risk become big problem for them is that they are afraid to pass through it and their altitude toward controlling it weather they would want to attempt or not.

Then, if this is the problem, the question they should be asking themselves, is:

How do I see risk?

And what are my altitude toward risk?

What are the factor and how can I use to approach it and put it under control?

And what really make risk to go up?

First can be classify into different level and size and they are:

1)   Individual risk
2)   Corporate risk
3)   Financial risk

Individual risk: All group of individual have risk of its own and the risk the fall into, most time, many of them don't even know the period of time when they are into risk or not.

Now you being in business by all yourself, without having proper financial statement and cash flow and income statement is a big risk of your own you include into, now you look into business into all the structure of your business know where to locate the area where the risk is great and you have take so much loan on the business putting the money into various side of your business growth then you sport the marketing area is not doing quite fine and the financial atmosphere is not good for your area to turnover of good profit to cushion the effect of the huge dept you own and it is having a big toe of your business growth. Looking back into your financial statement, is where all of this state from altitude, if you cannot control your altitude toward money your financial statement and income cash will look like this diagram.

Loan	Buying expenses car
Salary	Holiday
Business	More loan

→ Buy expense

Out from your treasuring to Another man treasuring

CORPORATE RISK

Business and enterprise go much further by seeing how to cleanup their corporate file and risk the to the berest minimum but are they totally free from risk?

Now coming to this risk can grap every side of their business growth if not properly manage there are so many organization that expose themselves so much into risk.

This are the factor that mostly push up corporate risk:

1) Executive loan
2) Income output is low to support business growth
3) Too much credit outside business circle
4) Financial atmosphere and policy too strict on business growth.
5) Market trend
6) If a business take too much loan to cover expenses can expose it to higher risk
7) Most business that is out of cash and need money to cover worker salary, operational cost, taking money outside with a very low output expose itself to risk.
8) If production output is low because market consumption of your business product is low can have a verse effect of your business growth.
9) Owing contractor too much can have an adverse effect on business growth
10) If the climate is not good for the business growth it can affect everything business development.

FINANCIAL RISK

This can kind of risk can be tame to be very worse if your money is inside it most of the business and enterprise put their money and asset in this classification.

Money change hand in most transaction and are carryout to but liquidity and other money making asset most time this type of risk is before mind by market trend and atmosphere policy at time if the market goes up you make more money, but if it goes down you loose all your money including all your investment. This kind of risk is very hard to control, because it is the market that determined the control and not you the individual

Diagram to show you flow fast risk grow to unprecedented level.

						60
						40
				Low market consump tion and low product	High operation Expenses And High tax	20
50 percent			Votile Atmos Phere and policy	Low income Output		15
	Too much to settle contractor					5
loan						0

If a business count to follow this trend it would be difficult for it to recoup his investment and it could be regarded to be on the high side of risk.

Votilibity of Market trend + With low consumer Consumption + Low Productivity + High operation expense

With too much tax = Risk

DOWN TREND
MITIGATING RISK TO THE BEAREST MINIMUM

Taking your risk into another new level should certainly have another new dimension but bringing it down to what you want take more of your sacrifice and effort then what you should urge to know is that, how do you approach risk? What major do you use to curtail it.

Maintaining risk involve half of the percent of your personal behaviour. If part of your behavior concerning financial aspect that can cause a bit of it is not control, it can spake it to grow.

I call it your sycological altitude toward money and maintaining on one single system and keeping that system to endure to yield the require result is what cause risk. Then, what do really need to do to bring it down, first and foremost, you should try to see on how you control it personally.

Since it involve all area of financial aspect, and for you to be under proper control of it, you should:

1) Implement a parameter to know the level of risk you are into
2) Implement good structural system on risk to control and bring down to certain level.
3) Implement good financial system on business to checkmate it.
4) Stop excessive wastage of money outside business cycle.
5) Implement good management system
6) Prepare against volatibity and atmosphere scene before it have adverse effect.

USED OTHER RISK INSTRUMENT AND INVESTMENT TO PUSH DOWN ON CORPORATE DEPT.

Corporate risk have his own spectrum and have his own way and tactic to bring it down, as we use other logical means to bring it down we may want to apply and consider other mean we can use.

Using investment instrument like, Federal Government bond or treasuring bill is one way we can use in bring down on corporate risk now this instrument being it long or short term investment with a period it take to mature and yield interest is a very good vehicle to use to cushion the effect risk might have on corporate body.

This investment instrument does include:
1) Federal Government bond
2) Treasuring bill
3) Commercial paper
4) Corporate bond
5) Private placement

Several instance and occasion through it liquidity office for those Federal Government issue his own bond to investor who may be interested to buy and with a gestation period it might take to yield interest and certify to pay in full to investor.

Corporate organisation or individual who might be deep into dept can buy into any of this instrument and use it to cushion the effect risk might have on their organization.

CHAPTER 4

MAINTENANCE STRUCTURAL AND MANAGEMENT SYSTEM

Any business that can be certify good or orderly must maintain it structural system. After stating the business, the first this he does is the administrative system, he put all administrative arrangement in place, but, how does it actualize that?

But how does his administrative system look like? Most people come up with their different style of administrative system.

But when your system is not good enough it would affect the foundation of the business from beginning to the ending.

Putting good system of administration have it long way to easing so many problem and the structure of the administrative system should be formatted this way and should look like this

Advisor – Directors
Leadership – CEO

When this structure of business is maintain and the helm of leadership is formulated in this way then it is easy to formulate law and principle to be implemented and executed the (CEO) mangoes executive director being at the top and helm of leadership formulate and draw a blue print on how the business should be run on a day to day basis and making sure that the business run and bring the desire output.

Most time he get independent advice from the executive director on how to chart a new way forward.

Each post and administrative department have his role to play in running a smooth business on a day to day basis. Member of staff and junior worker have their own role to play in executing the job pass down to them.

The system of business should look like this

Putting and actualizing this system is the best way to run proper administrative system on a day to day basis.

ACCOUNTING MANAGEMENT

Every beat of the accounting area have a role to play in detailing all aspect of money transaction carryout in that department and inside the organisation.

Putting up proper structural accounting system in place will save the company a whole some of money. Many organisation approach money way of putting their accounting book in order,

But how do you structure your accounting management to bring out the best from it

1) You must formulate and put in place all accounting system in place
2) You must know the inflow and outflow income cash flow
3) You must know the revenue the organisation generate
4) And must know the tax it is holding and urge to pay
5) It must have corporate account
6) Put all money made and outstanding into company account
7) Set it up from the top management level and take direction from the top on how the account should be run on a day to day basis.
8) Ultimate all system of payment, by using peetree and other accounting software in running the accounting system.
9) Set out policy and procedural rule to bring the best from the operational of the account.

AUDITING MANAGEMENT

Auditing all company asset, go a way to tell you what is a liability and what is and asset most corporate organization who also take part in auditing all their asset have come to understanding the real importance on why they should do so.

On which they come to understand that it save them more on the procurement side, trying to buy new asset for the business

Auditing all company asset will tell you all the complete item all asset that company is having at his disposal which might be off use or bad to the organisation. If any organisation is to bring out the best from it output and input he must regularly carryout proper audit on all his asset so as to enable it to know what is a liability to business operation and business need.

For a business to carryout audit.

1) It must put all system of auditing into place
2) Use independent auditor if the case may be, to carryout all his auditing need

3) Carryout audit to know what is a liability or and aseet.
4) Audit all financial aspect of the business, the inflow and outflow and excessing money coming into the business.
5) Audit all money owning and all taxes.

MARKETING MANAGEMENT

Formulate and putting all marketing system in place will help the organisation in driving his revenue base to a high sore.
Making proper structural marketing system its all it take to put you on the lead.

Marketing is divided into various special of marketing and they are
Medai Marketing
Distributorship marketing
Direct marketing
Partnership

Media Marketing is the firm of marketing that is being carryout on the social media, being it in the television, radio, bill band and most time the internet and other form of social media.
This form of marketing is one corporate organization use to capture the word of consumer and always using this medium to remind on the importance of using their product.
This form of marketing is every effective, because the al marketing this start from the mind and most corporate organization have use this tools in using a lost of consumer base for themselves on most time, it involve how you strategy to do that and on how you intend capture the mind of your consumer.

Distributor is another way you can reach your customer even more.
This form marketing involve the means of distributing your product by using independent distributor to help and carryout your product down to consumer.

Most organisation have benefit a lot by using this means of channeling their product to the end consumer.

Direct Marketing this is another great way you can use putting up you product to the general public most corporate organization employ good hand of marketer to help them to market their product to consumer and they have succeeded in using this mean to penetrate the market.

You can't use this method by employing good hand to market. For you so as for you to use the heart of your consumer.

Partnership forming partnership to drive to your marketing idea and conception is another way to put across your product to consumer.

Forming partnership with organisation that have the vision of your marketing idea with help in putting the right marketing tread in place now for you to be at best in marketing and drive corporate marketing goal, you must

1) Implement this system of marketing and put them into your corporate marketing goal and objective.
2) Develop and strategize in new marketing system if you must continue to win the heart of you consumer.

LEGAL AND ADVISORY MANAGEMENT

Putting all the legal system in place will help in easing all the area of legal matter corporate organisation go too much trying to solve or cut down on their legal related issue in which most time drag them deep into high legal cost.

Forming a department to take care of all their advisory and legal issue concerning genuine authentification, ajudification, corporate system, copyright law, legal disagreement between party and the general public will help bringing down company expenditure on legal related cost.

PROPER TAX MANAGEMENT SYSTEM

Any organisation who want to cut down on tax is to structure his tax management system so as to bring out the best from it.

Tax on his own have his own complex area and need proper care to put everything place and in order tax can be divided into two area and they are:

1)   Director tax

2)   Indirect tax

This two area of tax is what is being used today in administrate tax to coporate organisation and private entity

On most time, government on his own give tax break, to private entity who follow proper tax rule and proper organisation formation.

New organisation can implement their own proper tax system to include and document

1)   Income tax

2)   Product duty tax

3)   Procurement tax

4)   Corporate tax

5)   Transfer and other movement tax

By implementing and putting all this product into all proper tax system will save the organisation huge some of money trying to cut cost corporate tax and burden

CHAPTER 5

INCORPORATION

CUT DOWN ON TAX AND BURDEN ON THE WAY YOU REGISTER YOUR BUSINESS ENTITY

Now you have put all machinery in place and are gearing up to establish your business entity but how do you intend to register business name? you sat down reasoning on how to come up with that but do you know you can use proper legal framework to register your business and save the huge sum of money from tax and other expenses?

"Yes" there are ways you can use in register your business and minimize cost.

There are organization charge with the responsibility of doing that, and that organization is call (Corporate Affair Commission) most other country have their own organization that are responsible for that, you can register your business with this organization they will help you in defining the area where your business should be in the area of business industry and the area of business tax and with will also tell you to come up with your article of memorandum of understanding and they will want to know business location who are the shareholder director and trustee before they can register your business name.

Doing all this job by yourself might be daunting at time that is why need the services of lawyer to help you do the job for you so as to help you to minimize cost. Your legal advisor know the business entity that is good for you and will help you to register your business in the right format, tell your lawyer on how you want it to be register and he will help you out.

PARTNERSHIP

In which ever way you plan to register your business entity you must do it to give you the best result registering your business in form of partnership is another way to put your business name across.

Partnership entail that you are forming the business entity with somebody else, it could be your wife, brother, relative or friend meaning that, it is not only you or one person that own the enterprise.

This kind of enterprise setup have is own way government administrative tax to it and if a partner on the business setup die the business fall into the hand of the second partner and will still be running on business operation.

Two or more people bringing him resource together to form an enterprise means that the are limit that they can go up their enterprise together.

UNLIMITED

Forming and registering a business under this form fall under the level of production it is into the parameter use in asuparing the level of production tell well weather it a large or small company and the commit it can go

International organization that form into a sole entity will come in to register and put their business name under this format to save them on cost on tax to avoid either of full harm business entity.

CORPORATION

Forming this business entity and registering its name in this format tell you the parameter the business is into in the legal frame.

That when the need to put the right legal frame come by selecting this formation as business name

CHAPTER 6

EXPANSION AND PARTNERSHIP

Expand your business concept far and beyond will make you to meet the right target for your market, this is the only way you can pass across your business idea straight down to your client and consumer and all this going to be made possible by you carryout business expansion and partnership so as for you to drive up consumer volume and consumption but before you even think of doing this, you might want to consider:

1) Do you have the resources to open new office for your expansion?
2) Don't you have adequate man power to control and run this new offices?
3) And who are sole partner and how ready are they good to work with you?

Before ever think of expanding, you may want to consider, putting all machinery and tactic in place.

In each zone you decided to open an office, you must make sure is easily accessible, either by road, or train, to enable your good or product get your consumer.

Use adequate man power to man this offices and use other means and factor to drive your business idea and product to already made market.

FORM PARTNERSHIP TO DRIVE YOUR BUSINESS IDEA

Another way to do this is to conceptualize on this, by forming partnership.

Most corporate organization use this method in driving the volume of product sell to consumer and it has really aid them so much by allowing them to penetrate deep into the market and increase on product sale.

1) For you to penetrate the market even move you need to form partnership with your sole agent.
2) Implement partnership strategy into your marketing plan to drive your product consumption up
3) And welcome any new partnership plan into the over all

CHAPTER 7

TAKING YOUR BUSINESS TO PUBLIC DOMAIN

After putting finishing torching into the business and it has started running turning up income cash flow for you, but you still want to take it further by putting it into the public domain to get through to your patriot and consumer.

Then you instituted and formulate organization internal control and public relation to strengthen the mutual relation that you have with your customer the strongs bond that you have with your customer will always make them to remember your strong relation you have with them and will make them to remember you and patronize your services.

All internal control system must be put in place in checkmate all lapses and cement and bond all existing relationship you have with your customer.

INITIATE (IPO) INITIAL PUBLIC OFFER AND PRIVATE PLACEMENT

Playing the game of a real investor involve more merely by just setting up a business and wait for it to grow gradually, people who play this party trying to raise their corporate profile and organization are welly know to be expert and great investor who understand the business and investment train very well.

There are thousand of organization and business out there who never understand it and play it this way by taking their enterprise public.

Tack full most corporate organization use the medium to raise fund to settle understanding and use most of the fund for business expansion. I call this kind of investor ("the ultimate investor") because they know all what it take to bring out business out from corporate distress to stand out very strong.

And ultimate investor use his organization or enterprise by approaching the exchange to buy share and use his means to raise fund for his organization and shareholder.

It take as far as and instant for real investor to use this means of raising capital to complete unfinish project.

Before anybody can approach this means of raising fund, he must follow due process to complete the request.

1) The organization must approach the exchange (stock exchange) and meet on any of the issuing house to agree on the deal.

2) Put application or apply to the effect

3) Put on request of the allotment of share the organization may want to buy (at time it vary base on the type of fund intend to raise).

4) Most organization go through private placement to actualize this aim.

After meeting all the statutory requirement, he wait and see how the issuing houses put on his investment formality in place so as for the organization to meet or his investment objective.

ESTABLISH CUSTOMER DATABASE AND CONSUMER INDEX

Another good way organization can deepen it relationship with client is to establish follow up customer database and consumer index to enable it track the level of relationship it has with the customer.

The problem with most organisation is that they fail to put up proper index in place and in the caused that make them to loose a lot of customer. Because of the lack of index, most of them don't know how to improve or ajust to client need or want if an organization might be on the lead of customer relation he must put this system of index in place to enable it know the history of performance it have with customer, what need to be done, and how to improve on product and other customer need.

Consumer index is another system corporate organization can use to know the level or amount of customer and organization have, under watch eye, this is the area an organization can use to know the level of consumption of his product who is consuming his product, the level of history of customer, and how to track and improve on customer relation.

ESTABLISH CUSTOMER HELP DESK

Another way to bring forward strong customer relation and bond is to establish customer help desk as to help to take care of customer complaint and need.

For corporate organization to continue to win their heart and patronage they must take customer complaint seriously.

Your customer are like child to you, and always make them to feel welcome and don't for get that, this is mean you can use to understand their problem and they will be close to you.

CHAPTER 8

CORPORATE TAX SYSTEM AND INSURANCE

For you to put a formidable block and control on how you are charge on corporate tax you must have to formulate corporate tax system but how do know what to do so as to put the right system in place?

What does good corporate tax system involve.

Before you can even be certify good in the good tax management system your tax system must be reform so as to meet the present day need as well as meet international standard having it in the cause that, if it is far from solving present day need, then is good has not be implement at all.

Most corporate organization have continue to renew and update their tax system to enable it run smoothly and meet with the challenge of the present day need and those who find it hard, to put up their tax infrastructure are still lacking behind in the area of good tax management system.

Now before you can put this system in place, you may want to consider

1)   The implication for you and your business operation

2)   The cost implication and what you stand to gain from it

3)   Your area of competence in managing tax system

4)   And the control factor, what you need to do to put the control balance on check so that, it does not go up but fall to the bereast minimum.

Working and putting the system include:

1)   Personal income tax system

2)   Duty tax system

3) Operation and other running incur tax system

4) Corporate income tax system

5) Transfers and movement tax system

When all this system of tax is in place it will make it easy for you to manage and correct any abnormality that will come within it and put your corporate tax system in good shape.

DRAW A EASY BLUE PRINT ON MATTER CONCERNING TAX

In the course of establishing, you may want to define the way you want your corporate tax system to look like, that is when the need of overall plan come into place you categorize the system and put them into orderly.

Like the personal income tax system the system has his own define role and relatively dealth with worker or employee salary tax need.

It remove all bottle tie into scheme on how tax should be remove from their income and administer a proper framework on how it should be run.

DUTY TAX SYSTEM

This form of tax is another way tax is remove from load of goods.

If the load or container of goods is large, then there is a way government agency charge with the responsibility of collecting tax does it. It will use his parameter to measure and weight it, and this enable it to know the level of amount heavy duty of goods that are inside the load or container. Corporate organization set this system to check the cost of storing their or good in heaving duty load or container

OPERATION AND OTHER RUNNING INCOME TAX SYSTEM

This form of tax system is another way tax can be collected. Knowing the form of it operation, or weather it running in full capacity or at a very low range will determined the level of amount of tax that can be collected.

If the business income table is good running at a very low cost of expense with high capacity ratio of production, then the tax that will be place on it will be high, most organization have put up system to curtail cost to them

CORPORATE INCOME TAX SYSTEM

This form of tax include the overall income tax the organization is paying to government. If the enterprise is a large one it be documented and gazette to be large organization and the overall tax to it will be large.

But if the organization is indeed small government will want to know the level of production and capacity it can be able to handle before it can be able to place tax on it most small organization as small as they may be, can carryout production as big as large organization some enterprise setup their system to shield them from the overall cost and burden to them and their business.

TRANSFER AND OTHER MOVEMENT TAX SYSTEM

This form of tax is another way is being impost on corporate organization that transfer a lot of good or in the area of frequent movement of things.

Some organization has so many fleet and the cause of using and running them, from one location to another, incur a lot of tax from it.

The more this fleet are on the road, the more the tax on them.

That is why more organization are putting together proper movement and transfer tax system in place, to check the menace of the high tax of running the fleet and to control the expense to them.

USE INSURANCE TO COVER LOPE HOLE AND EXPERTED OCCURRENCE

The occurrence market is taking all form of the market and putting across their product to meet and across most corporate organization need and want

If you have not use insurance product before, now is the time to start to explore most of his product.

Organization can now start turning their attention into using or buy into their product to solve most of unexpected occurrence and problem. It is true most people don't like to insure their money.

Many other people have many other reason of saying so, for Christ sake, we should let good is changing, very fast, and the future and unexpected occurrence is blank, since we don't know how tomorrow look like, then we have to change our mind set and embrace insurance to solve most of our problem.

Insurance have come, has come to stay infact it is revolutionize the way we come to settle claim.

This is the time most corporate organization should start looking inward on how to explore different product that are found in insurance.

Insurance have nice product that cater for the need of corporate organization and personal need. It base on the one you are going for.

They are classify to include:

1)   Premium

2)   Silver

3)   Gold

And base on the claim you are looking for:

1) Life claim

2) Unexpected occurrence

3) Insure against the future

4) Insure against personal belonging

5) Insure against personal asset and liability

Knowing fully well that insurance cannot cover every claim

Organization that fail to implement this policy into their corporate file will have itself to blame for taking the wrong path

Organization should always think tomorrow and carryout everything it take to actualize policy.